Christmas Medleys for Two

4 Graded Duets for Intermediate Pianists

Arranged by
Wynn-Anne Rossi

Christmas is a special time of the year that unites faith as a community with family traditions. During this season, spirits are lifted by so many well-loved Christmas tunes that bring rich memories to mind. This collection combines the best of this music into unique duet medleys that celebrate the holidays. Through these duets, students can share the magic of the season by performing with a friend or family member.

Christmas Medleys for Two, Book 3 is arranged at the intermediate level with the pieces placed in the approximate order of difficulty. The arrangements are carefully graded for students yet retain the flavor and feeling of the original melodies.

Alfred Music
P.O. Box 10003
Van Nuys, CA 91410-0003
alfred.com

ISBN-10: 1-4706-2961-5
ISBN-13: 978-1-4706-2961-8

Cover art:
Christmas Tree: © iStock / Ellen Moran • Gift Boxes: © Shutterstock / Vitaliy Krasovskiy

WHAT CHILD IS THIS?/
UKRAINIAN BELL CAROL

Secondo

Arr. Wynn-Anne Rossi

"What Child Is This?"
Traditional English Melody

WHAT CHILD IS THIS?/
UKRAINIAN BELL CAROL
Primo

Arr. Wynn-Anne Rossi

"What Child Is This?"
Traditional English Melody

Lilting (♩ = 112)

Secondo

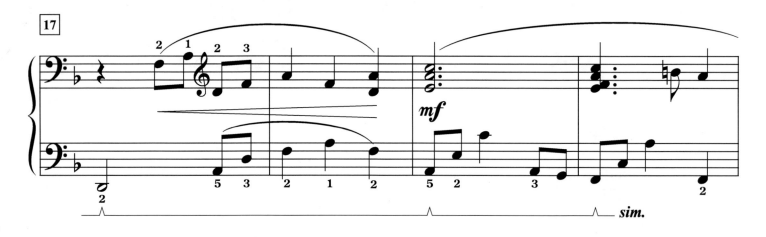

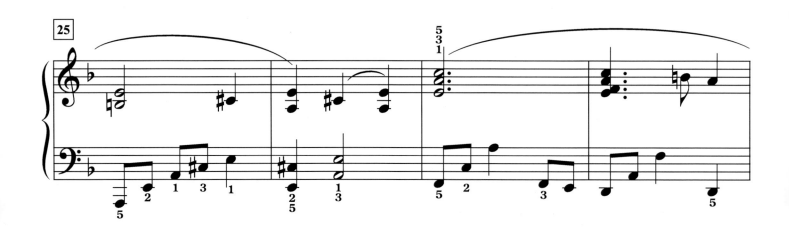

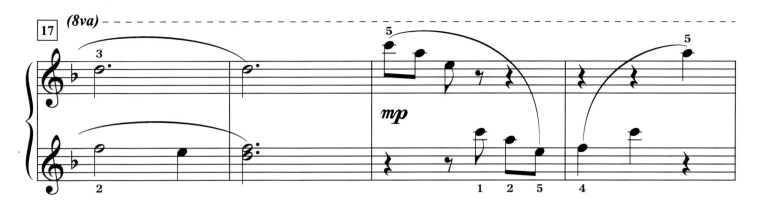

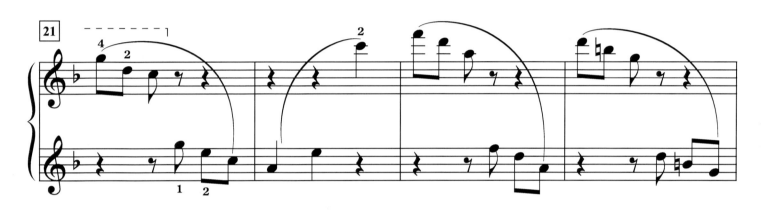

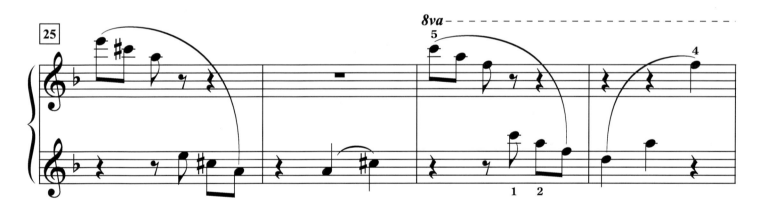

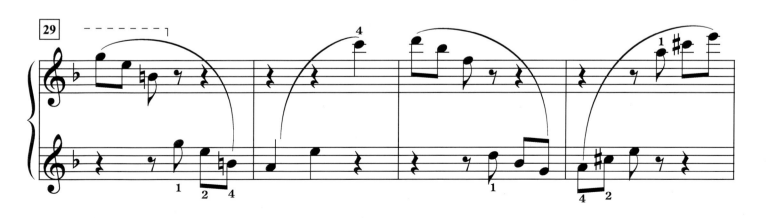

Secondo

"Ukrainian Bell Carol"
Mykola Leontovych

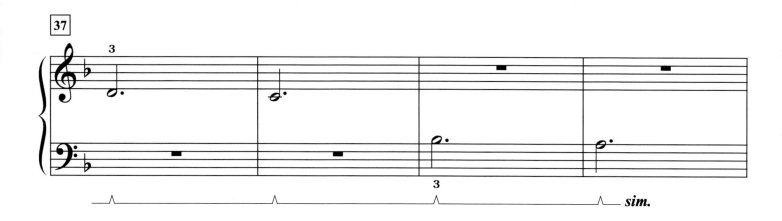

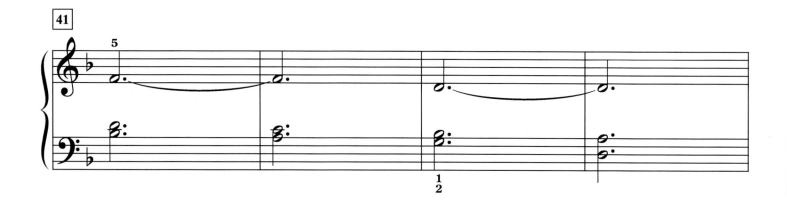

"Ukrainian Bell Carol"
Mykola Leontovych

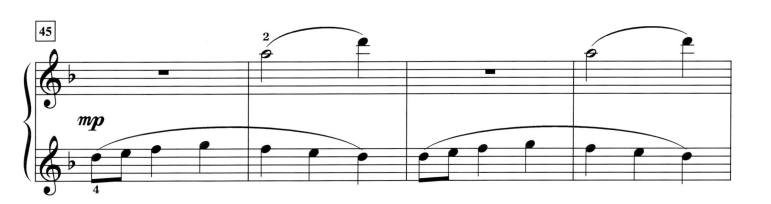

Secondo

DING, DONG, MERRILY ON HIGH/ HARK! THE HERALD ANGELS SING

Secondo

Arr. Wynn-Anne Rossi

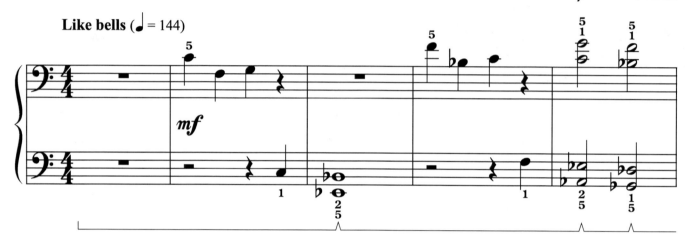

"Ding, Dong, Merrily on High"
Traditional French Carol

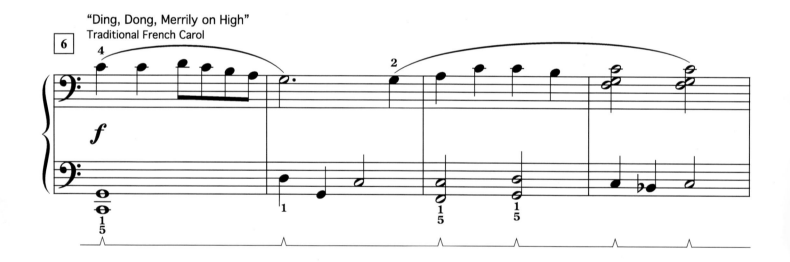

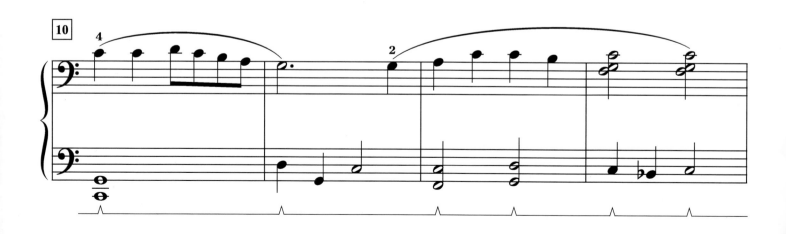

DING, DONG, MERRILY ON HIGH/ HARK! THE HERALD ANGELS SING

Primo

Arr. Wynn-Anne Rossi

"Ding, Dong, Merrily on High"
Traditional French Carol

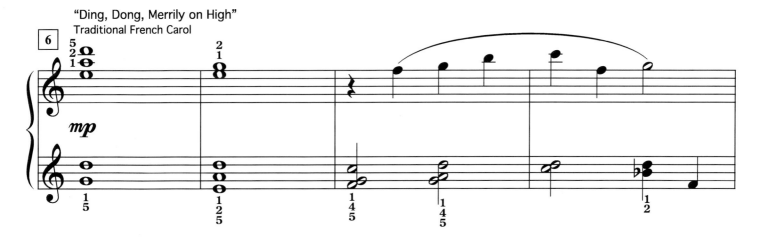

Secondo

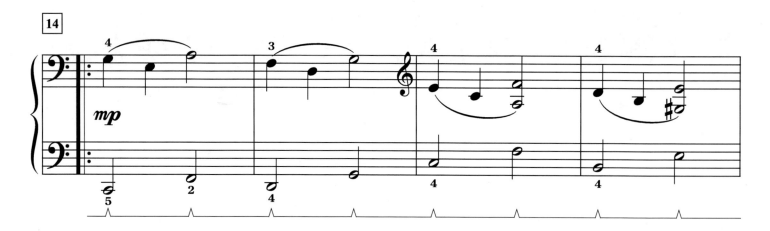

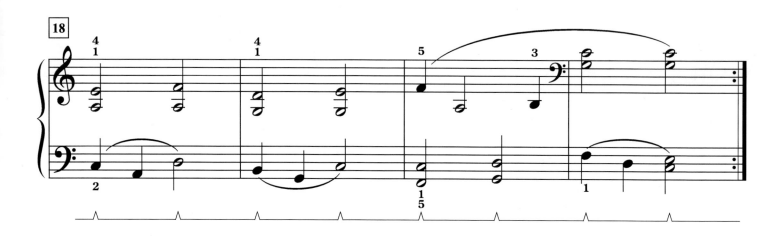

"Hark! the Herald Angels Sing"
Felix Mendelssohn

Majestic ($\quad$ = 132)

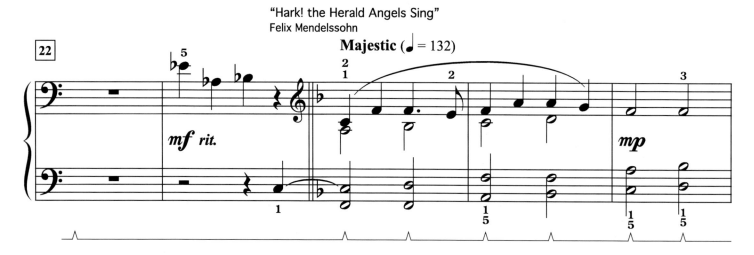

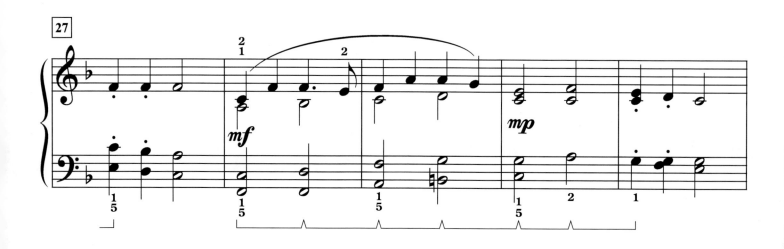

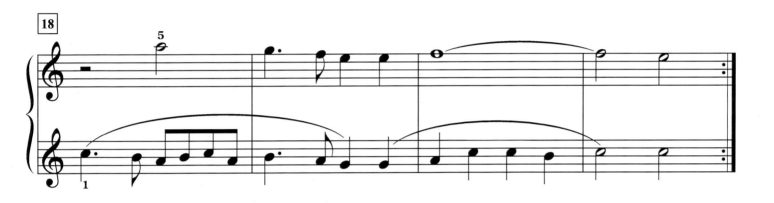

"Hark! the Herald Angels Sing"
Felix Mendelssohn

Majestic (♩ = 132)

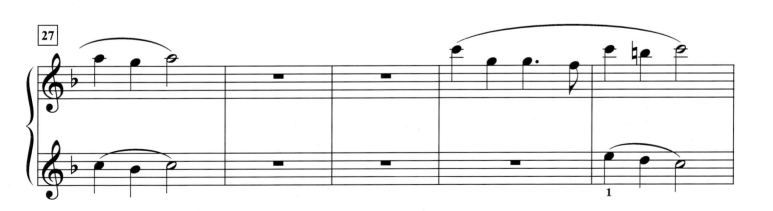

Secondo

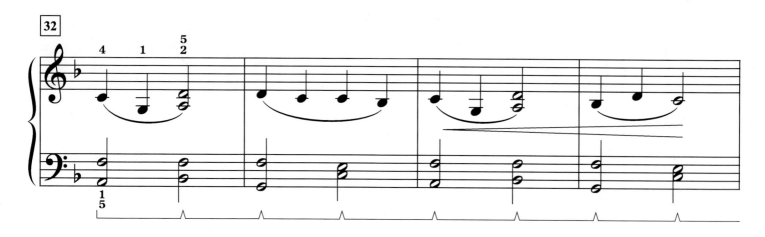

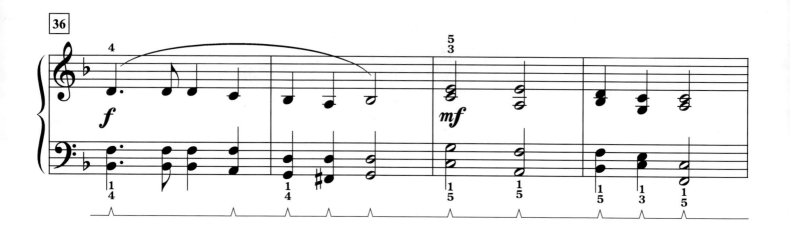

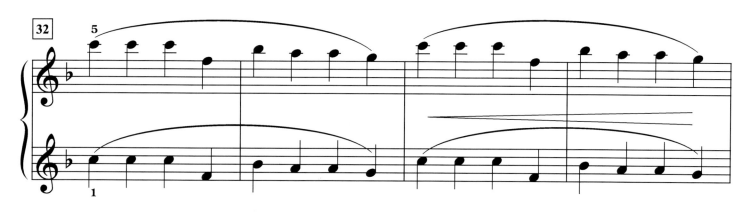

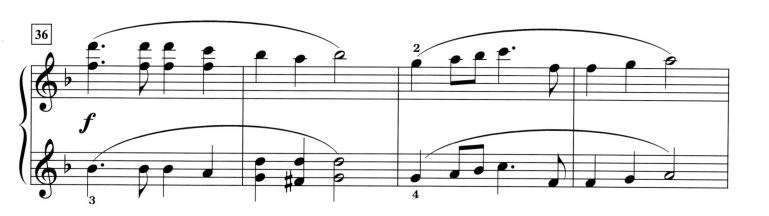

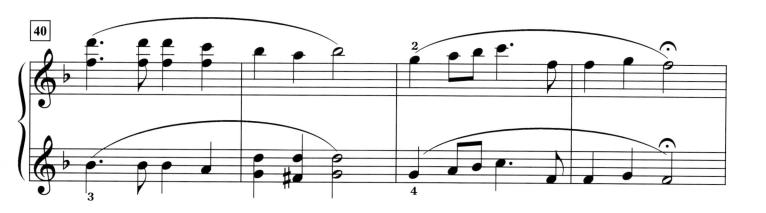

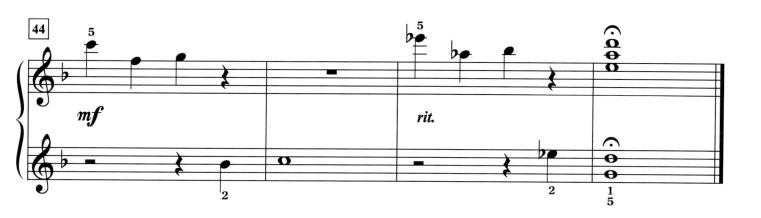

LO, HOW A ROSE E'ER BLOOMING/
IT CAME UPON A MIDNIGHT CLEAR

Secondo

"Lo, How a Rose E'er Blooming"
Michael Praetorius

Arr. Wynn-Anne Rossi

LO, HOW A ROSE E'ER BLOOMING/
IT CAME UPON A MIDNIGHT CLEAR

Primo

"Lo, How a Rose E'er Blooming"
Michael Praetorius

Arr. Wynn-Anne Rossi

Thoughtful (♩ = 52)

Secondo

"It Came Upon A Midnight Clear"
Richard Storrs Willis

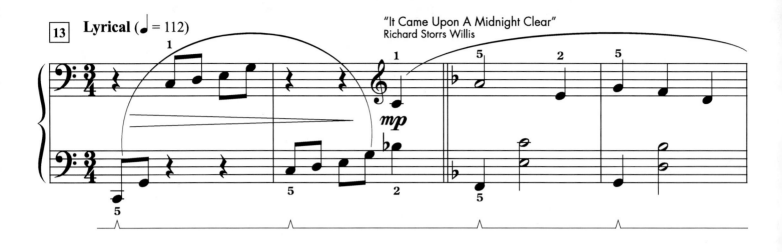

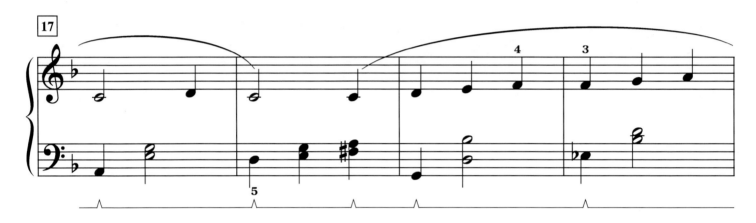

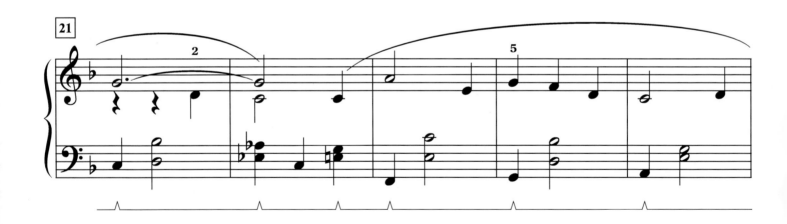

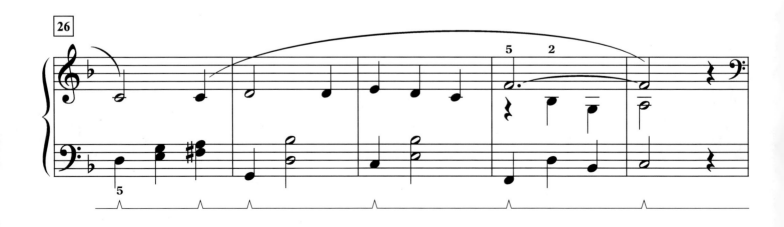

Primo

"It Came Upon A Midnight Clear"
Richard Storrs Willis

Secondo

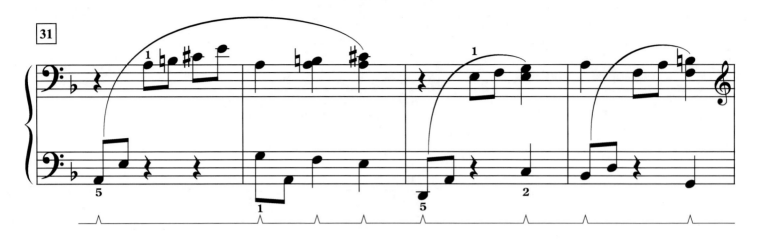

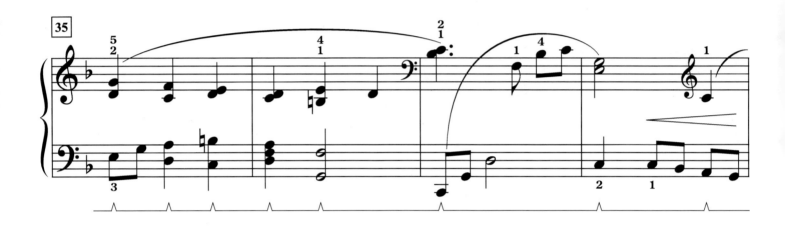

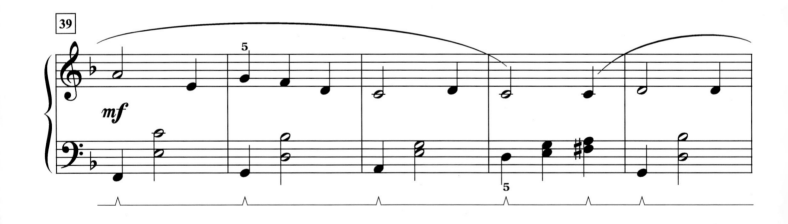

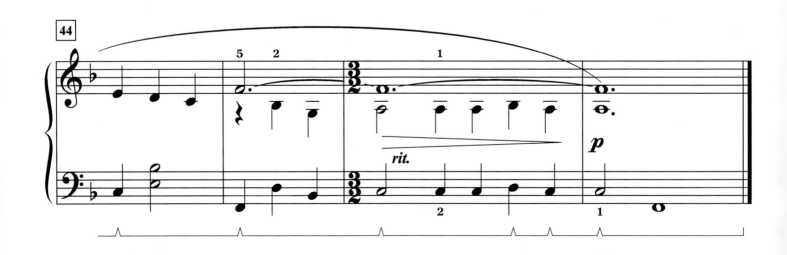

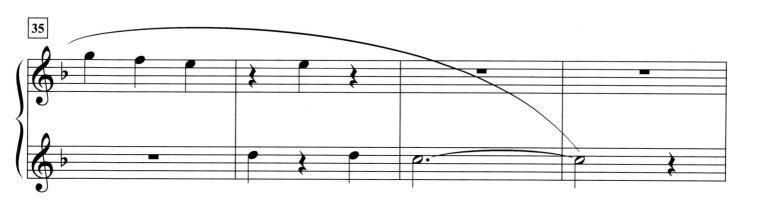

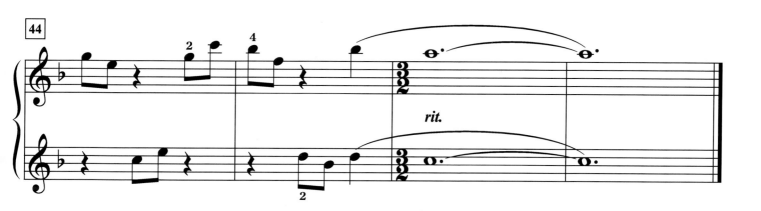

JESU, JOY OF MAN'S DESIRING/
O HOLY NIGHT

Secondo

JESU, JOY OF MAN'S DESIRING/ O HOLY NIGHT

Primo

Secondo

Secondo